The Story of California by May McNeer
Illustrations by C.H. DeWitt
Originally published by Harper and Brothers, New York, in 1944
© Reprinted by permission of the Estate of May McNeer

© Copyright 2020
Beautiful Feet Books, Inc.
San Luis Obispo, CA 93401
www.bfbooks.com
Revised and edited by Rea Berg © 2020
ISBN: 9781893103849 (pbk.)
Library of Congress Control Number: 2019954292
Printed in the United States of America

THE STORY OF
CALIFORNIA

LITHOGRAPHS BY C.H. DeWITT

TEXT BY MAY McNEER

Edited and updated by Rea Berg

NEW YORK   HARPER AND BROTHERS   1944

SAN LUIS OBISPO   BEAUTIFUL FEET BOOKS   2020

The Fabulous Land

Between the Pacific, whose surf washes its western shores, and the mountains of the Sierra Nevada which guard its eastern borders, lies California. Named for an imaginary island in an old Spanish romance, California is a fabulous land indeed. There you will find the country's coldest and hottest spots. Bodie, California has freezing temperatures over 300 days per year, and Death Valley can reach temperatures over 130°F! This inhospitable desert also boasts the lowest place in the United States, at nearly 300 feet below sea level. And Mount Whitney in the Sierra Nevada range is the highest peak of the lower 48 states. Within its borders, snow-crowned peaks look down on valleys fragrant with blossoms and on fiery deserts where whitened bones of animals lie near the graves of hardy adventurers who died there of thirst.

California not only boasts the tallest trees in the country, but also the largest and the oldest. Redwood trees tower so tall they seem to rise up into the heavens, and giant sequoias are so vast they weigh over 600 tons. But the bristlecone pine in California's White Mountains is the oldest tree with some pines over 5000 years old.

California has gardens blooming in the desert, farms and orchards that provide the fruits and vegetables for the nation, and vineyards where winemakers bottle vintages enjoyed around the world. Black oil pulses through miles of pipelines, huge factories hum with machinery, and technology giants continue to push the boundaries of invention.

Behind the varied and colorful California of today, stretches a history full of romance and adventure.

CALIFORNIA

Thousands of years ago, diverse tribes of Native Americans were the first to settle in California. Crossing over the Bering Straits, either by land or sea, scientists believe they were following big game like mammoths and mastodons. Here they found a land abundant with plant and animal life and they were skilled at identifying and harvesting edible seeds, berries, mesquite beans, piñon nuts, chia, cactus, agave, desert apricots, jojoba, barrel cactus, and holly leaf cherry. In their redwood canoes, they fished for swordfish, sailfish, shark, sardine, tuna, halibut, perch, sea bass, surf-fish, and mackerel. On land, they ate a diet of deer, rabbit, duck, salmon, bass, elk, trout, and quail. Their respect for nature enabled them to live in harmony with their environment and amongst the various tribes they generally lived in peace.

In 1542 a ship sailed into the Bay of San Diego. The Spaniards, who had conquered Montezuma's empire in Mexico, thought that by following the coast northward they would find their way to the South Seas. This ship, commanded by Juan Cabrillo, was trying the theory out.

Later, when Spanish galleons began making regular yearly trips between Manila in the Philippines and Acapulco in New Spain, they occasionally sailed along this coast. Once three Franciscan priests disembarked, said a mass on a hill, and claimed the land for Spain. Spanish sailors sighted or touched upon the California coast during the years that followed, but Spain was more interested in the riches of the Spice Trade than the wilderness of California.

One of the first explorers, and the very first Englishman, to set a booted foot on the wild coast was Sir Francis Drake, who sailed his *Golden Hind* into a northern bay in 1579. He called the wilderness New Albion, and claimed it for Queen Elizabeth. As he stepped warily up the shore of the small bay, with his men close behind him, Drake saw either Miwok or Ohlone Indians jogging toward him from a row of dome-shaped huts. The men were chanting, the women were wailing and slashing their faces–actions Drake assumed were signs of submission. In Drake's journal he recalled, "But we used signs to them of disliking this and stayed their hands from force, and directed them upward to the living God, whom they only ought to worship."

But Drake did not stay. For more than a hundred and fifty years the Indian nations of California were left in peace.

Spanish Mission Bells

Up from Mexico rode a man, small and ill, but with a great will and a strong purpose. He was Father Junipero Serra. With the courage born of a great dream, this Franciscan priest gathered his robe about him, mounted a mule, and rode into the unknown country to the north. He dreamed of conquest, not with the sword, but with the church protected by the sword, and he made his dream come true. During the next fifty years, he was to establish twenty-one missions along the coast of Alta California–through these he brought the white man's ways and religion to the Indians.

Even the mule track along which his mount slowly picked its way up stony hills and through brushwood, lived after him. This trail became known as El Camino Real, the King's Highway, and later as The Old Spanish Trail.

Father Junipero's first mission was established at San Diego. His expedition arrived there in two parts, one having come by sea, the other by land. Father Junipero chose to ride up overland from Mexico with the group driving the first herd of cattle into California.

Father Junipero started to work at once on his missions. He built them well. Around the church spread gardens and fields, and to Indian

herders guarding the mission cattle on distant grazing grounds, came the song of the sweet-toned bells in the church tower.

The native Californians came to the mission to watch the strange "white gods" at work; they remained to learn weaving, carpentry, and building. They built small irrigation systems, and in return they received clothing, food, and religious instruction. If they grew tired of prayer and returned to the wilderness, soldiers from the *presidios*, or forts, were sent to bring them back, and they were coerced into submission again. Over the years, the Indians were taught many things by the white men, but with their hunting grounds taken away, and their people decimated by European diseases, their traditional way of life was no more. When California became a Mexican possession, the missions were removed from the control of the church, and many Indians were left without the strength and unity of their former communities.

As Father Junipero's mule trails pushed northward, Spanish ranchers began to follow these trails, with titles to large grants of land in their pouches. Reaching his land, the Spaniard would build a simple adobe house and settle there with his bride. There the family would grow up, while out on the range their herds were growing too, enormous herds of cattle and horses tended by Mexican *vaqueros*.

These ranchers led quiet lives, enlivened by fiestas and rodeos, with dancing and riding and singing which lasted for days. They were prosperous and content, and they made laws restricting trade with other countries, to try to keep strangers out.

Occasionally a Yankee clipper from Boston dropped anchor in a California harbor. Then señoritas burst into joyous Spanish when they received clothing, household wares, and jeweled combs for their black hair. The men were equally glad to trade hides and tallow for plows and ranch supplies. But those ships, with their visitors from the outside world, came only occasionally, and for a hundred years the life of the Spaniards in California went on undisturbed.

Yankee Trappers

High in the Sierra Nevadas, American trappers dared the wilderness winters, seeking furs. Their search led them down the western slope of the mountains into the Great Valley, watered by two rivers emptying into San Francisco Bay. First to reach the Sacramento River, hunting

furs, was a trapper named Jedediah Smith, and his eyes popped in astonishment at the wealth of pelts he found there.

Russian fur traders, too, had discovered California. A group of them had come down from Sitka, Alaska, and built a settlement on the coast at Fort Ross. With them they brought some native Kodiaks and Aleuts. These Aleutians paddled their skin-covered kayaks along the coast hunting sea-otter, but they did not go into the valley for land pelts.

Smith located a headquarters for the Rocky Mountain Fur Company on the banks of the American River. Then he climbed back over the Sierras again to send in other trappers to take the rich furs. At Green River, which was a meeting place for trappers, Smith told marvelous tales of the "Spanish valley," and legend says, he opened a bony hand to show some pieces of metal that glittered in the firelight. He had picked up these golden nuggets near Mono Lake. But nobody thought much of them, for to the trappers wealth lay in fine fur pelts.

These Americans and French-Canadians cared nothing for the many laws forbidding trapping and hunting in California. The easy-going Spanish officials in their drowsy presidios could do nothing to stop Jed Smith and his friends from trapping in the Sacramento Valley.

The next year Jed and some companions went all the way to the Mojave Desert, and with careless bravado, on to San Diego. They were hailed before the governor for trespassing on Mexican soil. For California was now a province of Mexico, which had freed itself from Spain. The gold-braided Mexican governor ordered the ragged buckskin-clad trappers out of his province. So they made their way, living on the game they killed, up to the American River, where friends awaited them.

Jed Smith was never to find a fortune in either furs or gold. He died at last, this explorer of the West, slain by Indians, somewhere near Taos, New Mexico. But the Yankee trappers he had led into California continued to slip down over the Sierra Nevadas, carrying back loads of precious California furs.

Sutter's Fort

John Sutter was a restless, ambitious Swiss who came to America because he failed to make a living in Switzerland. He outfitted a wagon

with hardware, food, staples, and clothing and traded the length of the Santa Fe trail, with his shotgun handy for marauding Apaches and his old one-eyed yellow dog for company.

Sutter didn't talk much, but he saved his profits, for he knew what he wanted to do. When he had enough, he sold out his little business. Up the Oregon Trail he pushed along through heat and cold, buffalo stampedes and Indian raids, to Fort Vancouver. But at Vancouver he was disappointed to find that there were no ships going to California –which he had heard about from the Spaniards–so he sailed to the Sandwich Islands.

In the South Seas, John Sutter chartered the old bark *Clementine*, and loaded her with produce. He also took aboard a German cabinet-maker, who was ready for adventure, and ten Kanaka natives with their wives. They sailed to Sitka, Alaska, sold the produce there, then went on down the coast to California. Sutter talked the Mexican governor into giving him a large grant of land on the Sacramento River outside the area of the Spanish settlements. There Sutter watched his dreams come true.

He built an adobe fort to replace the grass huts the Kanakas had put up. The Fort became the center of a thriving little community, with shops, houses, and sheds. Hunters and trappers brought Sutter their pelts and enjoyed his hospitality. Sutter became a Mexican citizen and was friendly with everybody. His ventures prospered, and he visualized gardens and fields of grain and herds tended by Indians and Mexicans spreading over his vast holdings. He saw himself a virtual king in this wilderness.

He bought out the settlement at Fort Ross when the Russians decided to abandon it. Needing a sawmill, he had the machinery sent to him from the East, by ox-cart, across plains, deserts, and mountains. Near the present site of Sacramento, Sutter built his fort, called New Helvetia for his old home in Switzerland.

America from Sea to Sea

In a steadily growing stream, Americans were coming to the rich land beyond the high Sierras. The Americans liked California, liked it so

The Battle of San Pasqual, December 6, 1846

much that they believed it should be part of the United States. Being enterprising and energetic, these Yankees put thoughts into action so fast that the "new world" took shape in California before the Spanish ranchers realized what was happening.

The sleepy little capital town of Monterey woke one fine day to discover that it had surrendered to Commodore Jones of the United States Navy. This conquest, it developed, was a mistake on the part of the Commodore, who, while in Peru, had heard a rumor that Mexico and the United States were at war. With handsome apologies he sailed away again.

The taking of California would not have been so easy, even for the tough, tall men from over the mountains, if the Mexican authorities had not quarreled among themselves. Two factions, under Governor Pico and General Castro, spent their energies opposing each other. So when John C. Fremont of the United States Army, who had visited California in 1844 on a scientific expedition, returned a year later with a little band of soldiers, the Californians refused to worry. Fremont's intentions were obvious, but the Californians, content and prosperous, were concerned chiefly with their Pico-Castro quarrels.

Alarm was raised only when General Castro, in Monterey, heard rumors that Fremont had brought two detachments of soldiers to the Salinas Valley and Sutter's Fort. Fremont had few soldiers, but his trapper friends went to Sonoma, kidnapped the Commandant, and took the *presidio* without bloodshed. Then Fremont learned that the United States was really at war with Mexico, and the campaign became official. Commodore Sloat took Monterey without firing a shot, and San Francisco was soon occupied, too. Pico and Castro fled to Mexico, leaving a new flag of independent California, made of red and white flannel with a grizzly bear on it, fluttering above their old capital.

This flag was soon replaced by the Stars and Stripes, and Americans thought the war in California was over. But the Mexicans rallied, joined forces, and threatened to drive the invaders out until Colonel Kearney arrived from Santa Fe with reinforcements and saved the day.

California was purchased from Mexico by the United States for $15 million, and by that time wagon trains of new settlers were beginning to move across the western plains in regular procession.

The port of San Francisco in the Gold Rush of '49.

Off for Cal=i=for=ni=a!

When Jim Marshall told the other men working at Sutter's mill that he had found gold in the mill's tailrace, they laughed at him. Then Marshall took the handful of bright flakes to Sutter. Sutter, with his herds and fields, his shops and mills, had all he had ever dreamed of owning. He gave shelter and assistance to many of the arriving settlers, and sent out help to those caught in heavy snows in the pass. It was a pleasant world he had built, and he did not want it disturbed. He tried to keep news of the gold discovery quiet for a time. But in the spring the news leaked out and appeared in San Francisco's two weekly newspapers.

Gold! The word swept the little seaport town like a raging fever. Men hurried out to buy pans and picks and shovels, and left for the hills. San Francisco was emptied of its men almost overnight, and shops, homes, and farms were left to take care of themselves.

John Sutter's bewildered eyes saw his fields deserted by his Indians, Kanakas, and Mexicans. His horses and possessions were stolen. His fort was taken over by strangers. He could do nothing. The glittering fortune on Sutter's land ruined him forever, and started the greatest migration in human history. It was the Gold Rush of '49.

The big gold-mining areas of California were the slopes of the Sierra Nevadas, and the Upper Sacramento and the Klamath Rivers. To them the world turned frantic faces. There were stories of men who had taken out $100 a day, and sometimes twice that much, in placer mining on river bars. Steamship companies built up the legend of riches overnight, and some resorted to exhibiting gilded bars of iron as pure gold, to sell tickets to the West.

Every old tub of a vessel that could be made to float was crowded to the rails with whooping men, many of them carrying strange gold-

finding machines on their backs. Many ships took the long route around South America. Some poured out passengers at Panama to struggle across the isthmus through steaming jungles.

On the overland trails, Conestoga wagons rumbled and rattled westward in huge trains. Most of those who came in the gold rush were men, and they came on horses, on mules, in wagons, even on foot. "California or bust!" was their motto. They died of thirst in the deserts, of cold in the mountains, and perished in Comanches and Apaches raids. But more and more kept coming, and wild reports trickled back eastward as the gold fever mounted.

Towns and mining camps sprang up where there were no laws except those made by the miners. Provisions cost a fortune, and gambling halls raked in each night bags of gold dug in parching heat, in deep mud, or in freezing cold. Dutchmen, Chinese, Frenchmen, Yankees, Southerners, Australians—all came for gold. But only the sturdy survived.

Life was cheap, if food was not, in towns like Angel's Camp, Hangtown, El Dorado, Gold Run, and Sucker's Flat. A man would shoot a suspected thief in a saloon, then pass around a hat for gold to support his family. Claims were jumped, and men were shot for it. But miners preserved a justice of their own, and were generous to down-and-outers.

Those were the days of the forty-niners. After a time, panning for gold gave way to hydraulic mining, as big mining companies took the place of individual prospectors. Hydraulic mining, which washed away entire hillsides with high-powered hoses, swept mud, called "slickins," down to ruin farms and cause disastrous floods in the valleys. It started the mining wars in California, and was finally declared illegal. Dredging and machine-worked quartz mining were later methods; but the glamor of the gold-rush days had vanished long before they came into use.

Some of the old-time miners went back east, rich or ruined. Some settled on the land, and found new riches there. And some went to San Francisco, and found opportunities in a rushing, growing city as full of vitality as the spirit of the forty-niner himself.

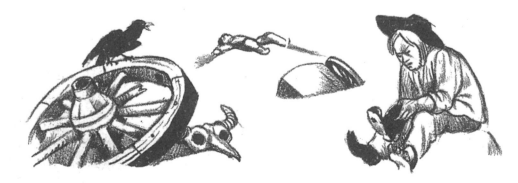

San Francisco

San Francisco was first a Spanish village, called Yerba Buena for the mint-like herbs growing on its hills, herbs used by the Indians as medicine. As the mission life declined, the settlement of Yerba Buena at the Embarcadero grew in importance, until with the discovery of gold it mushroomed into a city of tents and makeshift wooden houses.

Almost overnight the town was overrun with men who fought for provisions to take into the hills. The harbor was jammed with ships, many of them deserted by sailors and captain. And the town was crowded with miners from everywhere, spending their gold dust and then going back to the diggings for more. San Francisco, with its saloons and stores and wild, shifting population, soon outgrew the old law and order of the Spanish days. It was forced to fight crooks and highwaymen with a vigilante group until courts and jails could be established.

San Francisco grew rapidly because of gold; yet, when the production of gold declined, the city still grew. Its port is the finest on the Pacific Coast, and the famous Golden Gate is our western doorway to all of Asia. Silver, as well as gold, helped turn the city into a wealthy business center, for the silver mines of Nevada brought big mining companies to the port. This was the place where produce from the rich agricultural districts arrived also for shipment, and where the ship-building industry was becoming increasingly important.

San Francisco has always been an exciting town, and much of that excitement is there even now in the modern city, with its steep hills and cable cars, its beautiful and busy harbor, its cosmopolitan population. Even in the names of its three best-known hills the past and present are linked. Telegraph Hill was used long ago as a signal tower. On Russian Hill, Russian sailors were buried. And Nob Hill was named for "nabob" millionaires who built their mansions there in the years following the Gold Rush. San Francisco's Chinatown brings a colorful Far Eastern atmosphere into this most western city, but there is a reminder of Europe, too, in the city's large Italian section.

San Francisco has known peril. In the early days of the Barbary Coast on the waterfront, destructive fires raged through the wooden buildings. The fire known as the "Big Fire" came on the heels of the famous San Francisco earthquake in 1906 and consumed 28,000 buildings. Yet the city was rebuilt within three years with nearly 20,000 fireproof structures.

The world comes to San Francisco, and distance means little there. Californians like to plan big projects—and to carry them through. Two of the mightiest bridges in the world join the city to the mainland and span the Golden Gate. From San Francisco the path of the giant airplane "clippers" crosses the Pacific skies where the water routes of the old sailing clippers used to go. New York is only a brief journey away by plane, to the Californians whose fathers greeted dusty stage coaches from the distant eastern land beyond the great mountains.

The Golden Spike

For years, mountain passes echoed to the crack of whips and the shouts of mule skinners. Along the canyon trails, creaked covered wagons bringing supplies to the westerners and taking gold back east. Stage-coaches creaked westward filled with daring travelers, dusty and shaken up, but with guns ready for attacks by Indians and highwaymen. Ships filled with passengers and cargoes anchored in San Francisco Bay after long and perilous voyages.

But now speed was in demand. For more than a year, riders of the Pony Express, with mail pouches swinging at their pommels, galloped ahead of Sioux and Comanches across the plains to California. Then the telegraph line reached the western shores, its crackling wires bringing news so swiftly that the Pony Express was abandoned. And now came rumors of a railroad!

Ships arriving in San Francisco began to unload rails and equipment, and Chinese workers began the difficult construction of the railroad. The Transcontinental Railroad was built from two directions at once. Work trains started on the Union Pacific from Omaha, Nebraska, in 1864, and the Central Pacific built eastward from Sacramento, California, across mountain gorges. Builders advancing from Omaha had to bring ties, rails, spikes, and all the other equipment and supplies for their Irish laborers from Iowa. Most of the material used by the Central Pacific had been shipped around Cape Horn.

Construction trains on the plains were guarded by troops who fought off Indians as the engines pushed slowly westward. In the mountains, Chinese workmen built bridges and miles of snow sheds to prevent avalanches from burying the trains. But neither snow nor Indians could stop the pounding of sledge hammers and shouts of men at work. After more than three years the two crews met at Promontory Point, Utah.

A crowd was there watching, and in cities all over the Union, from San Francisco to New York, people waited. A silver spike from Nevada was driven into the last tie, then a spike of silver, iron, and gold from Arizona. A prayer was offered, and then blows from a silver sledge drove in the last, the golden spike from California. The blows of the hammer were carried all over the country by electricity, to ring bells in cities throughout the nation. A great shout arose across the United States, for from east and west the country was united. A band of steel linked the forests of New England to the monarch redwoods of California.

King of the forests

"Up north on the coast there are trees higher than a church steeple. There's enough wood in one of them to build a town!" Men who had been sent up to northern California to salvage a shipwreck of silk and tea, brought the news to San Francisco in 1851. San Franciscans laughed at the men's enthusiasm, but they never neglected a chance for profit. Within a year an engine and boiler were landed on the moist and foggy shore at Mendicino, and the first of many mills was set up to harvest the great redwood trees.

The redwood trees of California are like no other trees in the world today. These sequoias are the last of a family so old that they were growing on many parts of the earth when dinosaurs lived in a world of giant ferns. When the ice age came, only these trees withstood its rigors, and they died out everywhere but in California.

Some of the sequoias standing today are more than 2,000 years old, and were forest giants long before Columbus discovered America. They are of two kinds: the coastal redwoods growing in stands along the Pacific, nourished by the mists of the region, and the sequoias of the Giant Forest in Sequoia National Park on the western slope of the Sierra Nevada mountains. The coast redwood is taller; the mountain redwood is larger around the trunk. The world's tallest tree is Hyperion, a 379-foot coast redwood whose location is kept secret to protect it from harm. The world's most massive tree, also a redwood, of course, is the General Sherman Tree in Giant Forest, Tulare County.

The redwood forests are serene and beautiful, with a thick growth of ferns and flowers beneath the spreading branches. There is a strength and toughness, too, in the redwood tree that defies fire and insects. A forest fire crackling in the underbrush may scarcely scorch the old trees. Mighty winds can damage the monarchs, though, and when storms come the branches thrash about like prehistoric monsters snapping at each other. And when the lumberjacks fell a redwood tree, it crashes to earth like a descending hurricane.

In the early days, pioneers lived in hollow redwoods until they could build their homes, and sometimes they could construct five or six cabins from one great tree. Commercially grown redwood is used today for furniture, carved wood ornaments, and other things, but the finest of these ancient trees, priceless for their beauty and rarity, are now protected for the future in national parks.

Grapes to Eat—Grapes to Drink

The hillsides around California's beautiful Napa Valley, are planted with endless rows of grape vines. The first vineyards in California were planted by Franciscan priests at Mission San Diego de Alcala about 1770, and each new mission established its own winery. Later, men came from France, Hungary, Germany, and Italy to grow special kinds of wine grapes. The best wine regions are scattered along the coast valleys, in Sonoma, Napa, and Alameda Counties. Sweet wines come from the Fresno area, where raisins are dried in the hot sun, too. The old Guasti vineyard of Rancho Cucamonga, was built on land that was once desert, and at the time was the largest vineyard in the world. Its founder—Secondo Guasti—had arrived from Italy in 1893 with one dollar in his pocket. To provide for his workers, he built a school, fire station, bakery, a railroad, and a beautiful church.

In the past, whole families trudged into the vineyards to pick heavy purple clusters of grapes for the old stone wine presses which were built along the highways. Modern machinery has taken the place of bare feet, which were used for so many centuries to tread out the juice of the grapes. Grapes are dumped on an endless belt, stemmed and crushed in one operation, and dropped into troughs which carry them into fermenting vats. There is one vat cut out of solid rock, lined with glass, which holds 500,000 gallons. From the vats long lines of tank cars carry the wines to the bottling works.

When the harvest is in, grape growers celebrate their harvest festival with music and song. Floats roll through the streets, gaudy with tableaus as in old Italy. German brass bands follow them, and the festival ends with plays and dances in bright Swiss costume.

To Californians, California is the world—at least, there seems to be a small slice of everywhere in the world within its borders.

Golden Fruit

Oranges grew in mission gardens from the early days of California. Trees were brought there and grown at Mission Buenaventura as early as 1770. Soon they were being planted around adobe ranch houses. In the strong, sweet scent of the blossoms mustachioed señors serenaded their señoritas by moonlight. On drowsy afternoons ladies sat in patios

peeling small, juicy oranges as wedding plans were discussed. And the bride, kneeling in the mission chapel on her wedding day, wore–like stars in her black hair–the waxy blossoms of the orange tree.

At first, citrus fruits were planted as luxuries by priests and rancheros; as a crop they were of no importance compared with livestock. Mission priests had brought herds of sheep with them from Mexico, and taught the Indians to weave the wool. Americans coming west drove sheep and cattle before them across plains and mountains. Hides were called the first money of the Californians. But over the years, the value of livestock went down, and enormous fields of golden wheat covered the ranges. After a few more years, California farmers abandoned wheat and planted more and more vegetables and fruit, and the orange, grapefruit, and lemon became valuable crops. Today, citrus fruits bring to the state one of the biggest incomes of farm crops, and about 320,000 acres are planted in lemons, limes, oranges, mandarins, minneola tangelos, and grapefruit.

Water Magic

California's lovely valleys are indeed chosen places, but for many years in many other spots nothing but horned toads, cactus, and Joshua trees could flourish. These desert sands, bare and alkaline, had been death traps for man and beast for centuries. They had no water.

The early mission fathers had worked wonders with tiny irrigation systems. In the late 1800s California people began to think again about water projects, bigger and better ones!

Water can bring a magical change to a dry country which is without rainfall. Imperial Valley in Southern California was once a desolate waste called Salton Sink; now, reclaimed from the desert by irrigation, it is a huge garden of green vegetables which help to feed the nation. Early settlers thought of changing the course of the Colorado River to irrigate this desert. But when, in 1892, a canal was constructed, the river flooded and rushed into the dry sink, which then became known as Salton Sea. Many farms and settlements were swept away by the powerful waters. Again in 1905 and 1907 the Colorado River ran wild.

Then in 1936, Boulder Dam–later renamed Hoover Dam–was completed. This huge project controls the water of the All-American Canal

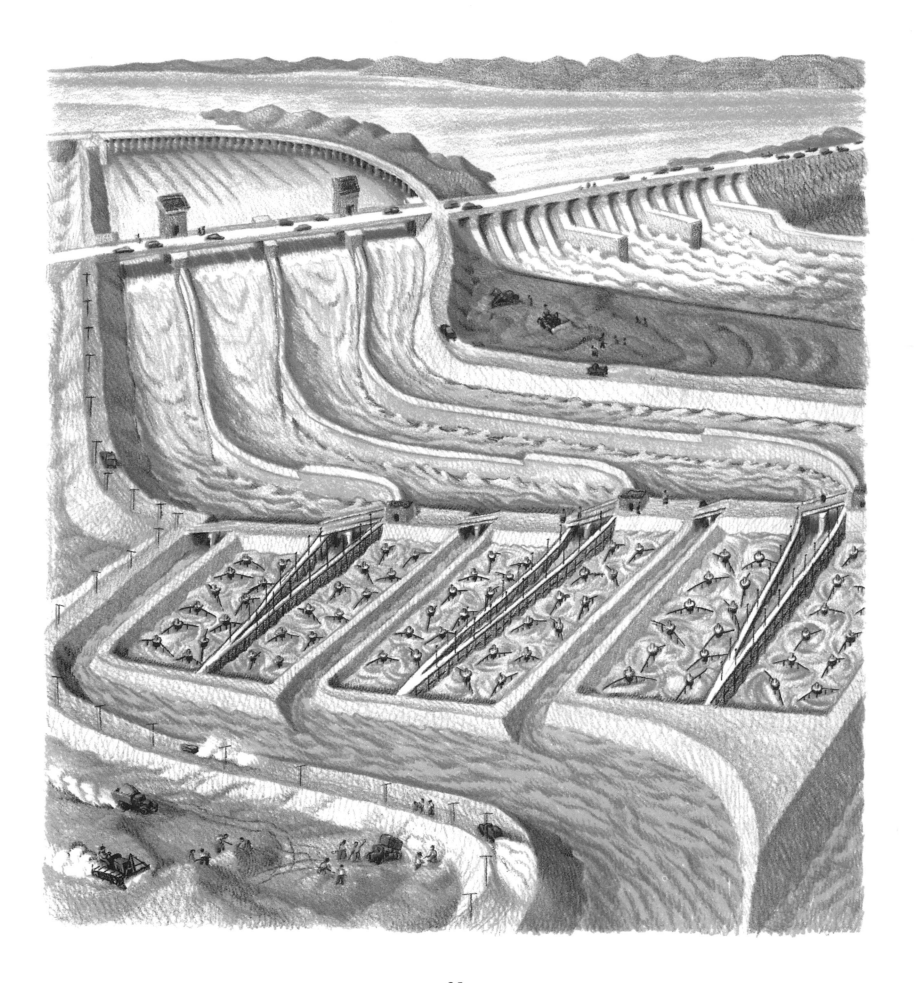

which was opened in 1938, giving life to the dry soil in the southwestern part of California.

The Colorado River has now been harnessed to its work, and its canal system has produced green fields and fruitful land–a new farming frontier.

In the 1960s, the California Aqueduct was built, beginning at Clifton Court Forebay in the San Joaquin Delta. It carries water from the Sierra Nevada Mountain snowpack, 444 miles to Southern California. The aqueduct supplies water for 25 million Californians and over 750,000 acres of irrigated farmland. Water–one of California's most precious natural resources, combined with man's ingenuity, has made life possible in the Golden State for countless millions of people.

Los Angeles

The city of Los Angeles covers 503 miles of Southern California, extending from the San Gabriel Mountains to the Pacific. The climate and facilities for work and play in Los Angeles have attracted people from all parts of the country. It is a farm town, an oil town, and a place of fashions, films, and airplanes. It is a city of many towns, of many nationalities, including the largest community of Mexicans outside Mexico.

The City of the Angels grew from a drowsy Mexican village to a noisy cattle market at the time of the gold rush. In the years since then it has become a place of factories and homes, with streets shaded by pepper trees and palms. Los Angeles has become the seat for a varied collection of religious sects, as well as for museums, art galleries, universities, and scientific institutions.

From the world of reality to the world of illusion, is only a step in Los Angeles. Inside many vast studios, you may see sets reproducing bits of almost any part of the world, and when the movie companies go on location and shoot their scenes out-of-doors, they make good use of the incredibly different kinds of scenery in the state. For Hollywood movies can duplicate many other countries without crossing California's boundaries. Sahara Desert films, with sheiks and tanks and airplanes, are made on the Mojave Desert, wild Indians yell and gallop after rocking stage coaches in the mountains, tropical scenes are taken on the southern beaches and islands, and the Sacramento River has doubled for the Yangtze and the Mississippi.

Hollywood draws men and women today–and children, too–westward as the bright vision of gold pulled adventurers in the days of '49. Hollywood seems too fantastic a place to exist. But it does exist, and, of course, in California.

El Dorado

Industrial development was slow in coming to California. There was no coal, and wood for fuel was scarce. There was oil–mission priests had seen pools of it on the surface and early settlers had smeared the sticky stuff on their adobe house roofs–but there was no market for it.

Then the mechanized age brought a wild rush for oil. Wells and refineries sprang up along the coast, in the San Joaquin Valley, and in other localities. There was a full-fledged oil boom, followed by a movement of heavy industry to the region.

This "boom" was typical of California's growth. People have always burst into it in hordes. California has always been, and is to many, an El Dorado, a land of golden opportunity. Since the days of the gold rush there have been booms, or get-rich-quick rushes, in real estate, in oil, in farming, and technology.

Thousands of landless farmers from the "dust bowl" turned to California. They believed that they could leave behind them poverty, dust, drought, and hunger, and find there a good life. They did not find it, for farming is a highly organized industry in California, and they could not break in. But eventually, other opportunities developed.

Aircraft is still an important industry in Southern California. And California is the leading agricultural state, producing over 400 different products, and the third-largest oil-producing state. From California endless miles of railroad cars and trucks move eastward with the riches of her earth and the produce of her people's hands.

California is a hard-working state, and at the same time it is one of the country's favorite playgrounds. Within this one state you can ski on snowy mountain slopes or swim in warm ocean surf. You can climb in rocky Yosemite Park or stretch out in a deck chair and watch the shifting lights on the sands of Death Valley. You can catch salmon at Monterey, tuna off Catalina Island. In Southern California you can have a magical adventure at the country's most beloved amusement park– Walt Disney's Disneyland.

National parks within the state include the Lava Beds and the Volcanic Monument in the north, majestic Sequoia Park with its aisles of giant trees, the Pinnacles Monument, Death Valley, and Yosemite Park. Yosemite Valley was carved out of the mountain by a glacier slowly moving down in the age of ice, as well as by the tumbling mountain streams. And Yosemite Falls is said to be haunted by the ghost of a Miwok Indian maiden who wandered too close to its lovely pool and was blown into it by a great gust of wind.

What Is California?

California today is a true "melting pot" of nationalities, trades, and cultures. It has Italian descendants growing grapes for wine, Portuguese running fishing operations off San Diego, Mexican farm owners in the Imperial Valley, and international shipping men in offices in San Francisco. There are the Scandinavian dairy farmers of Humboldt County, the orange ranchers in the foothills, and technology giants in the Bay Area.

California is home to the Chinese on San Francisco's old Barbary Coast, Korean immigrants running businesses in Korea Town, African-Americans teaching classes at university, and the great-great grandsons of Yankee sea captains who deserted their barks to hunt for gold. And in this beautiful melting pot, generations of Californians have mingled across diverse ethnic backgrounds, creating a mosaic of cultural richness unique to the Golden State.

California has proved an El Dorado to millions who can take the riches dealt out to them by lavish climate, soil, and natural resources, and work hard to supply the world with things it needs. Under the yellow, brown, pale, or sun-burned skins of California's sons and daughters, burn endurance, laughter, and an ever-ready willingness to take a chance on something new.

Biography

May McNeer (1902-1994)

In 1975 May McNeer and her husband, Lynd Ward, were awarded the distinguished Regina Medal for their lasting contribution to the world of children's books. Beloved author of such classic works as *My Friend Mac* (also known as *Little Baptiste*), May McNeer had her first story published in a Washington, D.C. newspaper when she was only eleven years old. McNeer was also the first female undergraduate student in her freshman class at the University of Georgia. She met her husband, Lynd Ward, while both were students at Columbia University, and they married the same week they graduated. They collaborated on numerous books, Lynd illustrating what May wrote. Their most well-loved book–*My Friend, Mac*, is the story of a friendship between a boy and a moose calf. Other collaborations included *America's Abraham Lincoln* (1957), *America's Mark Twain* (1962), *John Wesley* (1950), *Martin Luther* (1953), and *The American Indian Story* (1963). McNeer wrote *The California Gold Rush* (1950), *War Chief of the Seminoles* (1954), and *The Alaska Gold Rush* (1960), which were part of the Landmark Series. In the Regions of America series, May McNeer authored *The Story of California* (1944), *The Story of the Southwest* (1948), *The Story of Florida* (1947), and *The Story of the Great Plains* (1943). Each of these is illustrated with the glorious lithographs of C. H. DeWitt. *Armed with Courage* (1957) and *Give Me Freedom* (1964) are two more collaborations from the talented husband and wife team. Highlighting heroes and heroines of science, music, and humanitarian work, both books illuminate lesser-known individuals like Jane Addams, Albert Schweitzer, Marian Anderson, Father Damian, and Elijah Lovejoy.

C.H. Dewitt (1905-1995)

Cornelius Hugh DeWitt is beloved for the beauty of his lithographic work illustrating children's books. He was born in Cassel, Germany, on June 6, 1905, and spent his childhood and young adulthood in Europe, where he traveled extensively. In Paris, DeWitt worked in advertising to support his study of art at the Ecole de la Grande Chaumière and Alliance Française. In 1928, he emigrated to the United States. While working for the West Virginia Pulp and Paper Company, he became acquainted with Lucille Ogle, and soon launched a successful children's book illustration career with Ogle and Golden Books. His illustrations are featured in publications such as the Regions of America series including–*The Story of the Mississippi*, *The Story of California*, *The Story of New England*, *The Story of Florida*, *The Story of the Great Lakes*, and many more. A few of these were written by May McNeer, as is the one you hold in your hands. What sets these books apart are the exquisite lithographs, so lovely, that Barbara Bader, in her book *American Picturebooks* describes them as "intricately worked [with] the brilliance and subtlety of tones of work derived from artists' separations and the rich hand feel of lithography itself."

Restoring the work of DeWitt and McNeer–artists who devoted their talent and expertise to the world of children's literature–is an honor and privilege. Though the original text–at 75 years old–was outdated and in some cases, no longer accurate, it has been lovingly revised and updated for readers of the 21st century. The advances of digital technology allow for the reproduction of Mr. DeWitt's work so close to the originals that we believe he would be pleased and gratified with the results.

–Rea Berg, Beautiful Feet Books